Just a Book

Second Edition

Only one in a thousand people might benefit from the words of this book

That one might be you

But only if you read

CW00840335

To John

May the Lord richly bless you with His love.

Marius D Potgieter

Margaret S.

1

Published by: BESTME LTD

21 Woodside Close, Woking

Surrey GU21 2DD, UK

Available from Lulu.com and Amazon

© Copyright 2017

Marius D Potgieter

ISBN 978-0-244-01146-8

The Marvellous

The Greatest

The Kingdom

The Adversary

The Beloved

The Position

The Power

The New Dispensation

The Testimony

The Marvellous

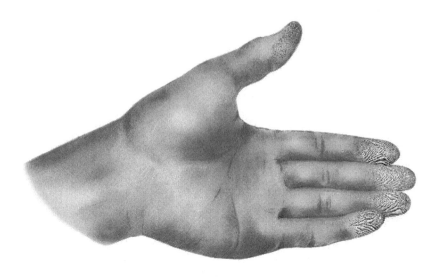

…each one of us his or her own unique fingerprint,

Do you know that you are marvellous? The fact that you are able to read and understand this writing is in itself a miracle. Written words and the images we view are transmitted through a clear adaptable lens on the front of our eye onto 120 million rods and millions of cones in the retina, then picked up by nerves leading to a specific area of the occipital lobe of the brain where we finally 'see'. This area is connected to other areas in the brain where these images are integrated and interpreted with auditory impulses that come from the inner ear via the auditory cortex. Isn't that wonderful?

Each organ of the human body is engineered to the finest detail from the top of our heads to the tip of our toes. For instance, the liver processes most of the nutrients absorbed in our gut; proteins, carbohydrates and lipids are metabolised in specific ways and many of these processes can be reversed as needed. And all this happens without us having to give it a thought. Who could have devised all that and made it happen? No man could have done it and, if you think about it, to ascribe it all to chance is downright impossible. Arguments in favour of this have been presented as man-made, sophisticated 'evidence' and are deferred to by most people, who seem to accept what they are told without really considering the absurdity of those claims. Be honest and ask yourself, how could all these marvellous things just have happened by chance?

What about your heart, which is a complex organ pumping specialised fluid – blood – to supply every cell in the body with nutrients and oxygen, normally contracting more than 3 billion times without rest in an average lifetime? And the wonder of our lungs? Also, the miracle of conception and a mother carrying a baby inside her body, fed via the specialised membrane of the placenta that separates her blood from her baby's, but allows gasses and nutrients to be exchanged as needed. And then after birth, by breathing air with oxygen, the baby 'changes' the mechanics of its own blood-circulation to become independent!

"For You formed my inward parts;
You covered me in my mother's womb.

I will praise You, for I am fearfully and wonderfully made;
Marvellous are Your works, and that my soul knows very well."
(Psalm 139:13-14)

One day, when we meet the Creator, He may very well ask us why we never gave Him credit for all the wonderful things – including nature and the universe – that He provided in order for us to be able to perceive His existence and seek to know Him. He even clothed us with skin, without which we cannot live, and gave *each one of us his or her own unique fingerprint*, all established at our conception by the marvel of our DNA. And still, He makes His sun rise even over those who do not believe in Him.

My faith in the Bible and what it teaches about eternal life hasn't always been this strong but over the years it has really grown on me, so that I now have absolutely no doubt about life continuing after death. If you believe there is just a small chance of it being true, is that not better than the alternative choice – nothingness?

There are numerous people with near-death experiences who have testified to this. Of course, those in denial of the truth try to explain these occurrences as natural phenomena, but they won't go away! For this reason, we should not live only for now. Our life on Earth is just a part of our eternal life, a preparation for eternity and a means to determine where we will spend it – either with Jesus or separated from the wonder of His presence.

When mankind decided to listen to Satan rather than to God, our spirit was no longer connected to the Spirit of God and instead of ruling our lives, became a rudimentary attachment of our soul. Three attributes of our spirit remain – our conscience, our seeking after God, and the conviction that life doesn't end when we die. Our conscience may be suppressed by continuing to do things that are wrong, but it never goes away totally. Seeking after God is universally observed, occurring in various ways from the most primitive of people to the most sophisticated. Lastly the spirit, rudimentary as it may be, testifies to us about the continuance of life after death. For now, we are one person; body soul and spirit.

Wonderfully, the Spirit of God can quicken written or spoken words from the Bible to become 'alive' and regenerate and nourish the human spirit so that we can 'see' and 'hear' spiritually and experience His presence. This happens as our spirit reconnects with the Spirit of God and helps us to understand Spiritual things. *The man without the Spirit does not accept the things that come from the Spirit of God, for they are foolishness to him, and he cannot understand them because they are spiritually discerned.*" (1 Corinthians 2:14)

However, many millions of people do communicate with Him spiritually and experience God's grace. Even so there is so much we will not be able to understand until after this life. *Now we see but a poor reflection, as in a mirror; then we shall see face to face. Now I know in part, then I shall know fully, even as I am fully known.*" (1 Corinthians 13:12)

Because God has made mankind in His image He wants them to be true to Him. *"God created man in His own image; in the image of God He created him; male and female He created them."* (Genesis 1:27)

Only God has the power to see and know all things with an eternal perspective, and it is through this knowledge and His teaching that He expects mankind to be able to discern good and evil. *"For with You is the fountain of life; in Your light we see light."* (Psalm 36:9)

This is the basis of universal order, which is based on God's will. God being the ultimate, supreme authority. He is perfect in righteousness and fairness. See what Moses, who had an intimate relationship with Him, said: *"He is the Rock, His works are perfect, and all His ways are just. A faithful God Who does no wrong, upright and just is He."* (Deuteronomy 32:4) He said this even though God denied him entrance into the Promised Land, because he hit a rock instead of speaking to it! One would think from a worldly point of view that this was unfair, this man Moses has given himself wholeheartedly, guiding more than a million people through the desert with great personal and family sacrifice, and now this one misstep and he won't experience the fruit of all his toil. God's thoughts and judgements are on a different level than ours, and Joshua, who points us to the resurrected Christ, took Israel into the Promised Land. This was something that Moses, representing the law, could not do. (See James 2:10)

But consider for a moment; if we think He is not fair, what can we do about it? Maybe say, 'we will refuse to follow Him.' Even so, He will still love us. But do you think that will make any difference to His power? Even if we can persuade a million people to think like us? All our arguments as to His existence or non-existence will not alter the truth!

God speaks to us by His Spirit through His Word, written in the Bible, which is the only true representation of His will and what is required of us. If you have never read it, I urge you to do so, but with an open mind. Why would the authors of the four gospels not be as reliable witnesses as any other who you do believe? Start, for instance, with the books of Mark or John or, if you are interested in a medical doctor's account of the way Jesus healed people and how He raised Lazarus from the dead, read Luke. *"…the beloved physician…"* (Colossians 4:14)

At this point we need some explanation as to what faith really is, and we find the definition in Hebrews 11:1. *"Now faith is being sure of what we hope for and certain of what we do not see."* Before sin interfered with the relationship, mankind and Creator communicated openly. After the fall, this changed and God made faith available as the only way mankind could reach Him. *"But without faith it is impossible to please God, because anyone who comes to Him must believe that He exists and that He rewards those who diligently seek Him."* (Hebrews 11:6) Faith, not imagination, was given as a way of communication between God and mankind. It replaced all our senses and anything we can improvise in order to communicate with God. It is also a test for true dedication. *"Jesus told him, 'Because you have seen Me, you have believed; blessed are those who have not seen and yet have believed.'"* (John 20:29)

Faith penetrates the barrier between the 'seen' where man lives and the 'unseen' where God lives – in other words Earth and Heaven. It works two ways; in faith we talk to God and by way of our faith He talks to us through His Word and with the soft whisper of His Spirit. This is the experience of those who believe and follow Him. Faith penetrating the unseen with Jesus as our Authority is the only God-sanctioned way. Jesus said *"I am the gate; whoever enters through Me will be saved. He will come in and go out and find pasture."* (John 10:9) *"I am the way, and the truth, and the life. No one comes to the Father except through Me."* (John 14:6)

Since the tower of Babel people have tried various alternative ways, such as witchcraft and fortune telling, to penetrate the unseen. These dangerous practices are condemned by God, and those involved bring a curse upon themselves, from which they have to be set free, before they are able to walk in power with Christ. If you want to hear about Jesus' faith in action and what He expects of his disciples, listen to this: *"The disciples woke Him saying, 'Master, Master, we're going to drown!' He got up and rebuked the wind and the raging waters; the storm subsided and all was calm. 'Where is your faith?' He asked them."* (Luke 8:24-25)

Did you know that in the beginning mankind was given dominion over all the Earth yet forfeited this gift when he listened to the Devil in the Garden of Eden? By doing this, he relinquished his God-given authority to Satan, became a slave to sin, subjected the entire human race to the same fate, and allowed chaos to enter the world with all the calamities to follow. It was this act of disobedience to God which led to our spiritual, and later physical, death. That sinfulness lives on in each of Adam's offspring, and the same sin that caused Adam to lose his fellowship with God lives on in our flesh, so we can't say we are suffering for someone else's sin. *"All have sinned and fallen short of the glory of God."* (Romans 3:23)

Why did God permit this? Because He does not want slaves who only worship Him from necessity or fear – He wants our love, and love can only be given as a product of a free will. So, He gives us a free will and that includes the freedom to sin. Yet, God gives us all the opportunity to turn back to Him through our repentance and obedience and, in so doing, receive His redemption. Have you ever considered accepting this for yourself? *"What good is it for a man to gain the whole world, yet forfeit his soul?"*(Mark 8:36) God loves us and will always welcome us, no matter what, because He *"wants all men to be saved and to come to a knowledge of the truth."*

That being said, once we decide to follow Jesus we place ourselves in a position to be tempted by Satan and his angels. He does it anyway, but more intensely when we come to faith in God. The attack takes different forms, from discouragement to outright persecution and mental oppression. There is a constant drip-feed of deception, should we choose to listen to it. Yet in all this we have the promise that God will give us the strength to overcome anything. *"They overcame him by the blood of the Lamb and by the word of their testimony, and they did not love their lives so much as to shrink from death."* (Revelation 12:11)

Another thing we have to understand clearly is that Satan carries the judgement of God upon him, and if we opt to follow him the same judgement becomes ours. God's love and judgement meet at the Cross where is found the only Hope of deliverance for the devil-infested and suffering human race.

The Greatest

"Go forth and stand on the mountain before the LORD." And behold, the LORD was passing by! And a great and strong wind was rending the mountains and breaking in pieces the rocks before the LORD; but the LORD was not in the wind. And after the wind an earthquake, but the LORD was not in the earthquake. 12After the earthquake a fire, but the LORD was not in the fire; and after the fire a sound of a gentle blowing. When Elijah heard it, he wrapped his face in his mantle and went out and stood in the entrance of the cave. And behold, a voice came to him and said, "What are you doing here, Elijah?"… (1 Kings 19:11-13)

Isn't it wonderful to know that it is possible for us as human beings to be acquainted with the greatest Being in the universe?
His name is God.

Let's think a bit about how wonderful He is.

He does not need to be elected because there is no one like Him.

He does not need to be replaced for He is eternal.

He has no room for improvement because He is already perfect; in love, in righteousness, in holiness and in power.

He has His throne in Heaven, the eternally holy place where nothing impure may enter.

He is the Creator of Heaven, of Earth and all that is in it. You need only look at the macro-cosmos and the micro-cosmos to have to admit that Someone great and wonderful must be responsible for such an intricate design. Not only the functionality, but the beauty of nature, of a song, of a person. If this is only an expression of His creativity, how much more wonderful is He?

There is now general agreement that there must have been a beginning to everything. Even if we were 'created' by a big bang and then the interaction of the environment, chance and natural selection over millions of years, who created the initial substance for all this?

"But," you may ask, "if God created all this, how was He created?" I would like to ask you a question or two in return. "The Universe – where does it start and where does it end? If there is some sort of border, what lies behind that border?" If you say, "Nothing" then you agree that there is no end. If we think like this about the Universe, we can try to understand a tiny bit about how great God is. He has no beginning, neither in time nor in space, and no end. *"Before the mountains were born or You brought forth the earth and the world, from everlasting to everlasting You are God."* (Psalm 90:2)

He is King over all.

"Lord, our Lord, how majestic is Your name in all the earth!" (Psalm 8:9)

God presents Himself as Father, Son and Holy Spirit. The Three of them are One as they share the same Spirit. Indeed, this seems to be a great mystery to some. How can God exist as three persons, yet One? Think of it as a lawyer, who is also a husband and father. Even God's children are included in the Oneness of Spirit; *"...all of them may be one, Father, just as You are in Me, and I in You, may they also be in Us."* (John 17:21) Because of the oneness of the Godhead, there is no question of polytheism. At the very beginning of the Bible we read about God, the Word and the Spirit.

God the Father is the centre and Head of the Trinity. He is the Greatest, the Magnificent, the Omnipotent and, by the Spirit, the Omnipresent. No one has ever seen Him, but Jesus *"...is the image of the invisible God, the firstborn over all creation."* (Colossians 1:15) And in John 14:8-9, *"Philip said, 'Lord, show us the Father, and that will be enough for us.' Jesus answered, 'Don't you know Me, Philip, even after I have been among you such a long time? Anyone who has seen Me has seen the Father.'"* This was when Jesus was on Earth representing the Father to us. When we come to Heaven, we will see Jesus at the right-hand side of His Father, and this incredibly wonderful, indescribable Father, Who is surrounded by unapproachable light, will now be approachable to His Christ-redeemed children. He is the Ultimate Authority and none can contest with Him – Satan tried and lost. Together with the Son and the Spirit He is everlasting and the origin of all life.

Hopefully by now you will have come to some conclusion about the existence of God, and understand some things about Him. However, you may ask, "Why can't we see Him? Why doesn't He talk back when I talk to Him? And why doesn't He do something about all the tragedies of this world?"

The short answer to all these questions is sin, astonishingly, a word many people do not like using nowadays because like hell, and even heaven, it is viewed as an old-fashioned idea. Without sin, there would not have been suffering. Not specifically sin of the one who suffers, but of humankind in general. When sin came into the world, man could not see God anymore or hear God anymore and because he had handed his God-given authority to rule the earth over to Satan, things didn't go well for the world anymore. That is why Christ had to die, to remove the sin that came between mankind and God. God's presence is still everywhere, but the difference is that the unbeliever cannot perceive it and the believer can. After judgement day there will come a greater divide; believers will live forever in the light of God's presence and the judged will join Satan in a place of total darkness away from the presence of God.

My dear friend who is reading this, and has not yet embraced God's salvation plan, time is running out and history is closing down on us. I am not trying to scare you, but if what is written in the Bible is the truth, and you are heading for disaster, how can I sleep at night if I do not warn you?

"Nation will rise against nation, and kingdom against kingdom. There will be famines, pestilences, and earthquakes in various places. All these are the beginning of sorrows." (Matthew 24:7-8)

Jesus wants us to make an informed decision to follow Him, so we have to know beforehand that persecution may follow our decision, and make up our minds not to fall away because of that.

Here are some Jesus' sayings relating to the Father. Nobody else who ever lived on Earth could say these words, and also be enabled by the Father to do the miracles which Jesus did.

"I came from the Father and entered the world; now I am leaving the world and going back to the Father." (John 16:28)

"For I have come down from heaven, not to do My will, but to do the will of Him who sent Me." (John 6:38)

"If you obey My commands, you will remain in My love, just as I have obeyed My Father's commands and remain in His love." (John 15:10)

"In that time Jesus, full of joy through the Spirit, said, 'I praise You, Father, Lord of heaven and earth, because You have hidden these things from the wise and learned and revealed them to little children. Yes, Father, for this was Your good pleasure.'" (Luke 10:21)

"'Now My heart is troubled, and what shall I say? "Father, save Me from this hour"? No, it was for this very reason I came to this hour. 28 Father, glorify Your name!' Then a voice came from heaven, 'I have both glorified it and will glorify it again.'" (John 12:27-28)

He even had a prayer for those who crucified Him, and divided among them the only possessions He had; His clothes. *"Father, forgive them, for they do not know what they are doing."* (Luke 23:34)

"'My food,' said Jesus, 'is to do the will of Him Who sent Me and to finish His work.'" (John 4:34)

Our 'food', like that of Jesus, has become to do the will of our Father. When people asked Jesus what the will of the Father is for us, He said, *"The work of God is this; to believe in the One He has sent."* (John 6:29). The Father testified about Jesus, with a voice from Heaven, *"This is My Son, Whom I love; with Him I am well pleased. Listen to Him!"* (Matthew 17:5).

The essence of doing God's will is therefore, that we believe in Jesus, listen to Him and obey Him. *"Enter by the narrow gate; for wide is the gate and broad is the way that leads to destruction, and there are many who go in by it."* (Matthew 7:13)

The One Who created man from dust offers you a relationship with Him. He is God, the Creator and Ruler of Heaven and Earth and the only hope for the remission of all our sins and the eradication of evil. He has an immediate and everlasting plan to rescue you – if you wish to be rescued. He does not send anybody to Hell; He gives each one of us the choice of whether we go there or not. When the Holy Spirit presents Jesus Christ to each one of us, via either the spoken or the written word, we make a choice either to accept or to reject Him as our Saviour – this is the choice I was talking about.

"Now choose life, so that you and your children may live, and that you may love the Lord your God, listen to His voice, and hold fast to him. For the LORD is your life…" (Deuteronomy 30:19-20)

The Kingdom

"Truly I tell you, anyone who will not receive the kingdom of God like a little child will never enter it." (Mark 10:15)

I cannot talk about The Kingdom without saying something about Heaven, because this is where the Kingdom's ruling centre or throne of God is. Heaven is in a totally different dimension to anything material; the most sophisticated radar or any other detector cannot pick it up, but it is more real and stable than anything we can think of. It is the template on which all we can see, hear, smell, touch and feel is based, just like the Earthly Tabernacle that the Lord showed Moses how to make was an image of the real Tabernacle in Heaven, as was the Temple that God showed David for his son Solomon to build. The paradise that was there at the beginning was just a material image of the heavenly paradise. *"And Jesus said to him, 'Assuredly, I say to you, today you will be with Me in Paradise.'"* Luke 23:43

Even our bodies are just a temporary abode for the real or spiritual people that we are. Paul likens our bodies to tents we inhabit on Earth and that we leave behind when we die. *"Now we know that if the earthly tent we live in is destroyed, we have a building from God, an eternal house in heaven, not built by human hands."* (2 Corinthians 5:1) We go to Heaven as spirit-beings. At the resurrection, we will unite with our new spiritual bodies, which will be like Jesus' resurrected body. God, who could make Adam from the dust of the earth, can certainly make our new bodies from our DNA or from whatever is left of our old bodies, or even if nothing is left as far as human tracing is able to detect.

"For nothing is impossible with God." (Luke 1:37)

Imagine God seated in Heaven with Jesus at His right hand and the Spirit visibly present, in the most amazing environment. The throne of God is there, and the crystal sea, surrounded by the most wonderful music and the real light of God, which is not restricted by speed or distance, like the light we know. And there is no shadow, or darkness, or sin, or sickness, or sadness or pain, and the angels and the redeemed who went ahead of us are all there!

Does this not make you cry out from the depth of your heart? **"I don't want to miss out on going to Heaven for anything I can have in this world!"** To use the quote Jim Elliott, 20th century missionary and martyr: "He is no fool who gives what he cannot keep, to gain what he cannot lose."

You can read a lot about Heaven in the Bible, and also in books written by people who have had near-death experiences, or those who have actually died and came back to life again. All tell essentially the same story about their experiences.

Jesus taught that His children are in this world but do not belong to this world, so where is their native land? As we read the Bible we often come across the phrase, "Kingdom of Heaven" or "Kingdom of God". When you are 'born' into the Kingdom of Heaven, where the throne of God is, this becomes your primary and permanent citizenship. Though you are most probably a citizen of a country on Earth, this is no longer where you are from. Your primary allegiance is to God's Kingdom and its ruler. Though we have to try and make the best of our time here on earth, we are just camping out on the way to our destination.

"Blessed is the man whose strength is in You,
Whose heart is set on pilgrimage." (Psalm 84:5)

The secrets of the Kingdom are there to be discovered by Jesus' disciples. He said, *"To you it has been given to know the mysteries of the Kingdom of God…"* (Luke 8:10)

This Kingdom is not one built by brick and stones nor can it be seen with the human eye. Rather it is an everlasting and spiritual home promised by a King Who ensures our victory over evil. The Kingdom transcends all kingdoms.

Strictly speaking no earthly country can be called a Christian country, as there are unbelievers in all countries, and people with other beliefs who do not adhere to Jesus' teachings. No one can really say they are a Christian and ignore the Great Commission, or fail to support those who obey it. A country would be nearer to being a Christian country if it dropped Bibles with parachutes onto other countries instead of bombs. This would cost only a fraction of the money of bombing and drones.

Off course you need to believe that the power of the Cross, is stronger than any earthly power. For instance, in the long term, it overcame the power of the mighty Roman Empire. And the real message of the Cross is not what the crusaders were practising! But I am afraid it would be far less politically correct to bring real hope to people in this way than it would to kill them and lay waste to their country. If you think that dropping Bibles from a plane would just lead to their destruction, let me tell you a story I once heard about a commanding officer in one of the closed countries who told his soldiers to destroy all the hundreds of Bibles they confiscated. When he asked, "Did you destroy all the Bibles?" his subordinate answered, "Yes, we saved just this one copy for you." Later the officer testified that he found Christ by reading that Bible.

Jesus said we must be innocent but also clever. What if you take a New Testament, in the dominant language of a specific country and, at the beginning, add some lovely pictures of that country and, at the end, Bible pictures that children can colour in and, when you open the back cover a few lovely Christian songs are played, with the words printed just inside? You may say that someone will make money by collecting these Bibles and selling them. Paul's answer to this is: *"What then? Only that in every way, whether in pretence or in truth, Christ is preached; and in this I rejoice, yes, and will rejoice."* (Philippians 1:18) Just for argument's sake, don't you think dropping millions of Bibles in Iraq, Afghanistan and Syria, would have had a better result than all the bombs and shooting? And all with no destruction of property or loss of lives!

Things we see with our eyes and perceive with our other senses all come from that which is unseen, spoken into existence by God. What we see is just an imprint of what is unseen, which will outlast everything we are able to observe now and is infinitely more wonderful.

It is possible for you to become part of God's Kingdom, to become an heir to His Kingdom, to receive wonderful blessings including the greatest gift of all, which is our everlasting communion with Him. We need this so badly that it should become the priority of our lives. *"Again, the kingdom of heaven is like treasure hidden in a field, which a man found and hid; and for joy over it he goes and sells all that he has and buys that field."* (Matthew 13:44) God grants us the weapons of this Kingdom – His words, which are sharper than any two-edged sword, and our faith, which is our shield. *"For the word of God is living and powerful, and sharper than any two-edged sword, piercing even to the division of soul and spirit, and of joints and marrow, and is a discerner of the thoughts and intents of the heart."* (Hebrews 4:12) The word of God generates faith, which justifies us to be filled by God with hope and with His love – agape love. *"Now hope does not disappoint, because the love of God has been poured out in our hearts by the Holy Spirit who was given to us."* (Romans 5:5)

Like faith, this love has substance, it is an experience, higher than feeling. It changes the mundane into exciting and makes it supernatural. It strengthens us through His teachings and commandments set before us. (Read 1 John 4:8-18 and John 13:34.)

Katherine Kuhlman said, "Love is something you do." I am sure Mother Theresa would have agreed with that! Love is also something sacrificial. When you love, you give something of yourself. It may be time, money or something inconvenient for you to do. If love is not your motivation, you will not keep on doing it. Love makes the distinction between people who may say they follow Jesus and those who really do follow Jesus. Those who only say, "Lord, Lord" and those mean it. (Matthew 7:21) The greatest sacrifice is your life, for instance a soldier who dies for his country. The highest sacrifice ever made was when the King of Heaven and of the Universe was prepared to die on an earthly Cross for us. Should we not be prepared to give up everything for Him?

The rule of the Kingdom, according to Jesus, is to love God above all, and then to love others like yourself.

The Kingdom of God does not flourish by any form of physical force or violence. *"'Not by might nor by power, but by My Spirit' says the Lord Almighty."* (Zechariah 4:6) In Matthew 10:34 Jesus said *"Do not suppose that I have come to bring peace to the earth. I did not come to bring peace, but a sword."* By this He meant that as soon as you become a professing Christian there will be a division between you and unbelievers, who will turn the 'sword' on you. Your life is going to be scrutinised by those who will try to ridicule you, manipulate laws to get at you, or even physically persecute you. These will include extremist humanists, atheists and people of some other beliefs and religions, with a Christianophobic attitude. Innocent actions like praying for someone will be seen as a serious offence. This is not a normal human response but is driven by Satan, who is behind the spirit of the Antichrist. There are numerous other anti-God thoughts and practices going on in this world, due to spiritual forces at work.

Remember Daniel? His enemies could find no fault in him, but turned on him because of his prayer-life. Joseph was accused of the very thing he managed to resist. It was his relationship with God that helped him to overcome temptation. *"How then can I do this great wickedness, and sin against God?"* (Genesis 39:9)

You do not have to be afraid, because *"He who is in you is greater than he who is in the world."* (1John 4:4) Just as Jesus was tempted tried and persecuted so too will we suffer the same fate. *"Remember, the word that I said to you, 'A servant is not greater than his master.' If they persecuted Me, they will also persecute you. If they kept My word, they will keep yours also."* (John 15:20)

The main features of Christianity are love and forgiveness. To love and forgive others sets you free. *"You have heard that it was said, 'You shall love your neighbour and hate your enemy.' But I say to you, love your enemies, bless those who curse you, do good to those who hate you, and pray for those who spitefully use you and persecute you, that you may be sons of your Father in heaven."* (Matthew 5:43-45)

"Beloved, do not avenge yourselves, but rather give place to wrath; for it is written, 'Vengeance is Mine, I will repay,' says the Lord." (Romans 12:19)

The struggle we face is not against any one person or persons, rather it is against principalities of darkness. *"For we do not wrestle against flesh and blood, but against principalities, against powers, against the rulers of the darkness of this age, against spiritual hosts of wickedness in the heavenly places."* (Ephesians 6:12)

*

27

WEAPONS OF OUR WARFARE

(From the notes of Charlie Wassell)

God provides powerful protection for our inevitable skirmishes with Satan. Ephesians 6:10-20 gives us a foundation for our beliefs about spiritual warfare and some powerful weapons we can use in battle.

[10] *Finally, be strong in the Lord and in his mighty power.* [11] *Put on the full armour of God, so that you can take your stand against the devil's schemes.* [12] *For our struggle is not against flesh and blood, but against the rulers, against the authorities, against the powers of this dark world and against the spiritual forces of evil in the heavenly realms.* [13] *Therefore put on the full armour of God, so that when the day of evil comes, you may be able to stand your ground, and after you have done everything, to stand.* [14] *Stand firm then, with the belt of truth buckled round your waist, with the breastplate of righteousness in place,* [15] *and with your feet fitted with the readiness that comes from the gospel of peace.* [16] *In addition to all this, take up the shield of faith, with which you can extinguish all the flaming arrows of the evil one.* [17] *Take the helmet of salvation and the sword of the Spirit, which is the word of God.* [18] *And pray in the Spirit on all occasions with all kinds of prayers and requests. With this in mind, be alert and always keep on praying for all the Lord's people.* [19] *Pray also for me, that whenever I speak, words may be given me so that I will fearlessly make known the mystery of the gospel,* [20] *for which I am an ambassador in chains. Pray that I may declare it fearlessly, as I should.*

BE STRONG IN THE LORD v10 - Paul begins with this command – we need supernatural power in this war Ephesians 1:19-22 and 3:20. In 3:16-17 Paul says 'I pray that God may...' followed by 'I pray that you may...' God does His part – we must do our part. We are to choose His power rather than our own.

Ephesians 6:12 mentions briefly 'the powers' - but the focus of the passage is on three things:

1. Being strong in the Lord who has overcome these powers;

2. Wearing our armour;

3. Remaining strong until the battle is over (Revelation 2/3).

THE WHOLE ARMOUR OF GOD – armour that our spiritual enemies cannot penetrate.

Romans 13:12-14 "put on the armour of light" – clothe yourself with the Lord Jesus Christ:

1. Belt of TRUTH – truth directly opposes Satan the father of lies. The battlefield is often our minds. The enemy plants all kinds of doubts – false ideas about God/ourselves/life. Truth helps us see through false beliefs and values.

2. Breastplate of RIGHTEOUSNESS – righteousness is our coat of mail. Because of what Jesus has done for us, we are right with God – now and forever. Once and for all He has removed our sin and guilt (Romans 8:1; 2 Corinthians 5:21). We are alive with the righteous life of Christ. When we believe this and rejoice in it, Satan's accusations will glance off our 'breastplates'.

3. Gospel of PEACE – peace is our protective footwear. In OT when Israel's army had won a battle, a runner would hurry to report the news of victory and peace. We are equipped with far better news: Christ's victory over sin and Satan (Colossians 2:15; Ephesians 1:19-21). Jesus has won the war! As we learn how to proclaim the news that God offers forgiveness and a relationship with Him, now and forever, we are able to set people free from Satan's control.

4. Helmet of SALVATION – salvation is a victorious word that embraces our past, our present, and our future. We have been delivered from the guilt and punishment of sin (John 5:24) we are being delivered day by day from the power of sin (Romans 6/8) – in the end we will be delivered from the very presence of sin. This hope of salvation (1 Thessalonians 5:8) gives us the certainty that God has a magnificent future planned for us. This hope, this confidence is not a luxury; it is a basic necessity for overcoming the enemy. Without it we might be disheartened by the enemy's frequent attacks.

5. Shield of FAITH – the faith of the Son of God (Galatians 2:20) – simply believing what God has said, including - Satan and his defeat - how to glorify God, even in the midst of trials and struggles - about Himself, His Son and the Holy Spirit, who fills us with power for obedience and service – about ourselves – how God sees us. Praising God is a way to strengthen faith – Psalms 145-150

6. Sword of the Spirit – WORD OF GOD – the Spirit's sword is sharp and full of living power (Hebrews 4:12). For maximum effectiveness as soldiers, we must become experts in using our sword. Jesus is our model for using God's written word as a sword for deflecting the devil's attacks (Matthew 4:4-10). We too can use scripture in our spiritual warfare – verses we have memorised. Then in the battle, the Holy Spirit can bring them to mind in a special way.

In prayer walking the Holy Spirit may give 2 Chronicles 20:15 'do not be afraid or discouraged... for the battle is not yours, but God's'. Or Isaiah 49:24-25 (NAS) 'can the prey be taken from the mighty man, or captives of a tyrant be rescued? Thus says the Lord even the captives of the mighty man will be taken away, and the prey of the tyrant will be rescued; for I will contend with the one who contends with you, and I will save your sons'.

PUTTING ON THE ARMOUR – there are no shortcuts, no simple formulas, for using the armour. We must let the truths of God's word grip our hearts. Read, study and learn God's word so that the rich and personal meaning can soak into our hearts.

PRAY AT ALL TIMES IN THE SPIRIT – Paul points us to another mighty weapon - warfare prayer (Ephesians 6:18). Prayer is God's heavy artillery in the battle against the invisible spirits who war against our souls and against God. C S Lewis wrote – God is calling us all to take part in a great campaign of sabotage. Prayer lets us operate behind enemy lines, softening resistance, confusing strategies, cutting off supplies, defeating evil purposes.

Prayer gives us constant opportunity to be on active service in this spiritual war.

Pray the Word of God (as in 6. above). It strengthens our faith – transforms our prayers into powerful weapons – fixes our eyes on God.

Pray in Jesus Name – we approach the throne of grace on His merits, never our own; we resist the enemy in His authority and his alone. Jesus name is not a magical word – it stands for decisive truths about who He is and what He has done – His infinite power and love – His triumph through the cross and resurrection – His reigning position, high above all other powers.

So that we don't misuse the Name of Jesus read Ephesians 1:19-21; Colossians 2:14-15; Revelation 12:9-11.

As we pray let us focus our prayers on God's purposes and glory.

FEARLESS PREACHING – in the final verses of this passage in Ephesians 6:19-20. Paul sums up the whole purpose of our prayer walking – that the evangelists can open their mouths and words will be given to them to proclaim the gospel fearlessly.

*

The rule of the Kingdom of God is superior to Satan's rule of the Earth. For instance, world history is going the way of Bible prophecy and neither Satan nor mankind can change that. Even Jesus adhered to the prophecies about Him. The Kingdom that reigns in the hearts of all true believers – though its physical presence remains unseen – is more real than any worldly kingdom and breaks through openly into the physical world at times.

The world puts up a strong resistance against the breakthrough of God's kingdom. For instance, you decide to talk to someone about Jesus, but just can't get around to talking to him, so you decide it will be easier to give him some Christian literature, but when you see that person, thoughts come to your mind like: "It's not the right time or the right place," or "It will intrude in the conversation," or

"He will be offended," or "He looks as though he's in a hurry," and then he will be gone without his tract and you will feel awful. But God knows your heart and does not stand ready to punish you; like the Father He is, He encourages you and gives you another chance, or there may be someone else who will talk to that person. To deny Jesus in front of others is a different matter and like Peter did, will need deep repentance to restore your relationship with Him.

Other examples of the breakthrough of the Kingdom are supernatural manifestations like those on the day of Pentecost and later revivals, healings and the supernatural protection that we sometimes experience. For instance, one can be as good a driver as it is possible to be, but still experience moments when our concentration may lapse and there could be an accident that does not happen. This occurs in many other areas of our lives as well, though for some reason, which we may only understand later, it sometimes does not happen.

Jesus represented the Kingdom all the time. He ministered under an open Heaven. *"Verily, verily I say unto you, hereafter ye shall see heaven open, and the angels of God ascending and descending upon the Son of Man."* (John 1:51) Manifestations of the Kingdom in the physical world are carried out by the Holy Spirit, usually as a response to prayer. For instance, the revivals were all preceded by the fervent prayers of believers. Jesus himself, even as Son of God, spent much time in prayer. When our prayer, penetrates the cloud of unbelief which is over us and also in our hearts, it creates an opening for our faith to go through, and we receive to the measure this happens. Faith or a lack of it was the issue why the disciples could not drive the demon from a possessed child, but apart from encouraging the child's father to believe, Jesus also stressed the importance of prayer (Read Mark 9:14-29).

Faith is therefore our supernatural connection with Heaven or the unseen Kingdom. It penetrates the unbelieving cloud that covers countries and nations, especially those that once had a strong Christian presence but have turned their backs on it. After penetrating this barrier our faith goes right into the throne room and the presence of God.

There is great power in prayer when it is done in the Spirit and with faith. It is a spiritual power which can move mountains; one which is greater than any other Earthly force or unholy spirit. And the wonderful thing is, we do not have to be physically strong in ourselves for God to use us to release His power! We need only have faith, based on God's word. With our prayers, as a spiritual force, we surround, support and protect those for whom we are praying.

As Christians, our proof lies in historic facts, faith in the word of God, and hope in the future. It is by His knowledge and teaching that we learn to pray as Jesus taught us:

"Our Father in heaven, hallowed be Your name,
Your kingdom come, Your will be done, on earth as it is in
heaven. Give us today our daily bread.

And forgive us our debts, as we forgive our debtors.
And lead us not into temptation, but deliver us from the evil
one.
For Yours is the Kingdom and the power and the glory forever.
Amen"
(Matthew 6:9-13)

In the Lord's Prayer, Jesus encourages us to pray to the Father that His will be done on Earth as it is in Heaven. As we do God's will, we become part of the fulfilment of this prayer.

The Adversary

"For the accuser of our brothers and sisters, who accuses them before our God day and night…" (Revelation 12:10)

Angels are God-created spirit beings, of whom Lucifer was probably the first. He was so great in his own eyes that he became proud and sought to challenge the King's authority and became an angel of darkness, Satan, God's adversary.

"How you are fallen from heaven, O Lucifer, son of the morning!
How you are cut down to the ground,
You who weakened the nations!
For you have said in your heart:
'I will ascend into heaven,
I will exalt my throne above the stars of God;
I will also sit on the mount of the congregation

On the farthest sides of the north;
I will ascend above the heights of the clouds,
I will be like the Most High.'"
(Isaiah 14:12-14)

Dishonoured Satan was cast away from God's presence with one-third of the other angels following him. With their support, he formed the kingdom of darkness to wage war against God's Kingdom seeking to sabotage God's creation, giving his full attention to the deception of mankind, who is created in God's image, which Satan hates. When he persuaded mankind to listen to him rather than to God, the image of God became distorted due to the sin inherent in every human being since. The God-given authority of mankind become that of Satan and humans became his immediate subjects – although God still reigns over all, as the Earth belongs to Him with everything in it. Satan's misappropriated authority will finally be taken from him when Jesus returns.

If we look around us and see just how badly many of us treat one another, it becomes clear that there is something unnatural and unholy at work; a 'designer of evil'. Satan and his spiritual troops are very real; they do not mind, however, that people deny their existence, as this means that they can work undercover. The demonic spirits under Satan's control are constantly at work on the minds of humans, manipulating us into doing the will of Satan, which is in direct opposition to the will of God. They are like spam email which you should delete without opening, but which are often cleverly disguised as something legitimate.

Fortunately, the Holy Spirit that lives in us is much stronger than these unholy spirits, who are afraid of us when we walk in His power. They are, however, on the lookout for any opportune time to catch us off-guard. His aim for Christians is to get them to commit a sort of spiritual suicide and his next goal is then for them to kill themselves bodily before they are able to restore their relationship with God. If not that, he keeps encouraging them to walk away from their faith. *"Be alert and of sober mind. Your enemy the devil prowls around like a roaring lion looking for someone to devour."* (1Peter 5:8) *"He was a murderer from the beginning, and does not stand in the truth because there is no truth in him. Whenever he speaks a lie, he speaks from his own nature, for he is a liar and the father of lies."* (John 8:44) Remember, one of the greatest lies the devil ever told is that Hell doesn't exist. Hell, most certainly does exist as the place of incarceration and punishment for Satan and his followers, and according to the Bible it will be deeply unpleasant to accompany him there.

Because spirit – life – is indestructible, including the human spirit, it is not possible to eliminate spiritual beings, only to relocate them.

It is through deception that Satan offers temptation to pervert our souls, coax us into sin and thus enslave us. He, and those he uses, may appear to us to be good and fair; *"And no wonder, for Satan, himself masquerades as an angel of light. It is not surprising, then, if his servants masquerade as servants of righteousness."* (2Corinthians 11:14-15) He hates every human being, even those who follow him he will in some way try to destroy, because all humans were created to the image of God. In the Bible, Paul reminds us that our battle is not really with flesh and blood, as with human conflict, but rather with forces of evil that continually oppose us whenever we seek to do the right thing.

Satan's kingdom had to be defeated, and God's honour restored. Judicially, Jesus has accomplished this defeat through His death on the Cross and resurrection. Though he is on the run, Satan tries to contend the validity of this verdict. Yet for all his doings he has already lost the battle, as there is no higher authority than God to turn to. Knowing full well his defeat and judgement Satan is forever trying to exert himself in as many ways possible against God and His Kingdom, until his time, set by God is over. As Satan is the master of lies and deceit, he may even deceive himself – and others – that he can still succeed against God.

The Beloved

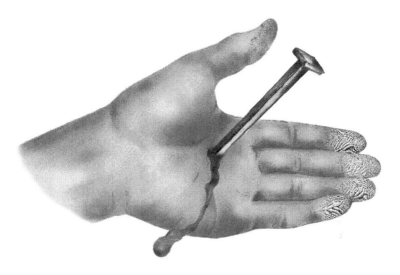

God's salvation plan for the human race cannot be ignored, or regarded as something unnecessary. He was prepared to let His Son die for it. What else can be more important?

What many people do not realise or want to hear is this – you have to be saved during your life here on Earth to be able to go to Heaven when you die. Only you can make the choice to accept God's salvation plan and have your broken relationship with the One, who is more wonderful than any person, restored.

The coming of Jesus into the world had been announced on many occasions by the prophets of the Old Testament and is clearly documented in the gospels. Jesus came to us through the Jewish nation, and in particular through Mary who became pregnant by the working of the Holy Spirit.

Jesus, the Son of God also became the Son of Man. Mary was called "highly favoured" by the angel who brought her the message that she would become the mother of God's Son in human form. She was a very special person; a young woman who had dreams of marriage to Joseph and bearing his children, and who would be accused of unfaithfulness when she was obviously pregnant before the marriage. Yet she said to the angel: *"Behold the maidservant of the Lord! Let it be to me according to your word."* (Luke 1:38)

There is, however, no mention in the Bible that she will obtain a supernatural position alongside Jesus. On the contrary, Jesus clearly indicated her place on the same level as other believers when He said, *"For whoever does the will of My Father in heaven is My brother and sister and mother."* (Matthew 12:50)

Central to the Christian message is this: Jesus Christ is not just another prophet or messenger, He is God Himself Who came to the world in human form. *"Jesus said to them, 'Most assuredly, I say to you, before Abraham was, I AM.'"* (John 8:58) He is thus called both the Son of God and the Son of Man. As one of the Godhead, He came to represent the Father. Though He was crucified, He has risen from the dead and returned to Heaven from where He will return. All authority in Heaven and on Earth has been given to Him. He is King, Priest, Prophet, Saviour, Brother, Friend and Servant to all who believe and trust in Him. *"All things have been delivered to Me by My Father, and no one knows the Son except the Father. Nor does anyone know the Father except the Son, and the one to whom the Son wills to reveal Him."*

(Matthew 11:27) He lives within and among us through the Holy Spirit.

One thing we cannot obtain by just being the best person possible is our salvation. Jesus has accomplished this on the Cross, where God's demand for uncompromising righteousness was matched by His unfailing love. To stand upright in His presence can be achieved by no other means.

Even if you do not yet believe in the God Who presented Himself in the flesh as Jesus Christ, consider how remarkable it is that one man along with a handful of fisherman and a few other people could have so many devout followers. This lowly man, the son of a woman not even fifteen years old when she carried Him, and Who was only trained as a carpenter, divided history into BC and AD.

Glory to God, Who gives us victory through what His Son has done for us, and by His Spirit Who dwells in those who believe and follow Him. The Devil has been condemned for orchestrating the murder of an innocent Man on the Cross and we await God's final judgement on him and all his followers. Disobedience which leads to sin is the reason for the suffering of mankind and separation from God.

We know that not only does God love us, but that He first loved us even before we believed in Him and, greater than that, He also loves all those who do not yet acknowledge Him.

By carrying that Cross, Christ paid for the sins of the whole world. Having given everything *"Jesus cried out with a loud voice, and breathed His last. Then the veil of the temple was torn in two from top to bottom."* (Mark 15:37-38) The way to God is now open.

According to John, the words of that last cry were, "It is finished!" He knew this was going to happen and He went through Gethsemane for it, and all that followed. He suffered for the sins of humanity as Son of Man, forsaken by God. He did it for you and for me – can you accept that?

When you consider how His coming into the world was the fulfilment of many prophesies, His life and the miracles He did; His suffering in Gethsemane and on the Cross, which He predicted; His resurrection from a sealed tomb; the many eye witnesses who saw Him alive and going to Heaven, with His promise to come back at the appointed time, don't you feel like saying with me, "I believe that Jesus is the Son of God"?

His sacrifice is an immeasurable gift for the redemption of all, but only appropriated by those who choose to believe and follow His teachings. *"Then Jesus spoke to them again, saying, 'I am the light of the world. He who follows Me shall not walk in darkness, but have the light of life.'"* (John 8:12) Only by accepting that Jesus Christ is the Son of God and following His teaching can we be saved. As Moses led God's people, out of the slavery of Egypt, so Jesus Christ leads His people out of the slavery of sin.

God's salvation plan for the human race cannot be ignored, or regarded as something unnecessary. He was prepared to let His Son die for it. What else can be more important?

The Bible teaches that there is no person without sin except Jesus Christ. Therefore, there is no one who can stand in God's presence without first asking for forgiveness which was achieved through the death of Jesus Christ on the Cross. The believer then stands before God 'in Jesus', His beloved Son, and so becomes one of His elected.

By reciting the following words from your heart, you too can become an heir to the Kingdom of God and experience the transforming power of the Cross and resurrection of Jesus:

"Jesus, I know I am a sinner, because I have rebelled against God, and I repent of this, and of every other sin in my life, that You will reveal to me now and in future. I realise that I cannot save myself, but I pray that You will save me. Thank You that there is no one too good or too bad for you to save. I believe that You died on the Cross for my sins and that God raised You from the dead, so that I can live with You. I declare before Earth and Heaven that You are Lord, Jesus, and I want to acknowledge You as my Lord. I want to follow wherever You lead me."

You now have the assurance that Jesus has brought you out of eternal death to eternal life. Congratulations! A very significant change has happened in you; the Spirit of God has regenerated your spirit, which was dead in sin, to become alive. Your walk of faith has started! You may or may not feel its effect immediately because this newly-born spirit needs time to grow. For some that growth may occur quickly, while for others it may take some time, but if you follow the guidelines in the rest of this book and its Biblical principles you will gain the spiritual strength and perseverance to withstand the trials and temptations which lie ahead. Believe me, something so wonderful has happened to you that Jesus said: *"...there is joy in the presence of the angels of God over one sinner who repents."* (Luke 15:10)

And now you have become part of the promise made to everyone who is called upon to follow Him. *"For I am persuaded that neither death nor life, nor angels nor principalities nor powers, nor things present nor things to come, nor height nor depth, nor any other created thing, shall be able to separate us from the love of God which is in Christ Jesus our Lord."* (Romans 8:38-39)

As Christians and heir to God's Kingdom we are commanded to walk upright and in the light of His Word. And through our faith and obedience we become citizens to this inheritance; our names written in the Book of Life where nobody can erase them.

By His grace, God gives us faith. Without faith, it is impossible to reach God. If you have faith, and believe, it's like going through an open door to discover the wonders of God's Kingdom. *"Jesus answered and said to him, 'Most assuredly, I say to you, unless one is born again, he cannot see the kingdom of God.'"* (John 3:3) If you have prayed the prayer, you have unlocked the door and find yourself in a place where the words of the Bible and all the Spiritual truths will become yours. *"And you shall know the truth, and the truth shall make you free."* (John 8:32)

You are sure to say, "I didn't realise that my eyes have been so closed to what God wants to teach me!" Yet you have only touched the tip of the iceberg, as there is so much more to learn and experience, and there will always be things beyond your human understanding. You are now seen by the Father as *'in Christ'*. Hallelujah! And to resist the encroachment of the opposition, you need to build your life as a sanctuary or temple for the Holy Spirit to occupy, where no evil spirit can claim a space. *"...your body is the temple of the Holy Spirit, Who is in you, Whom you have from God, and you are not your own. For you were bought at a price; therefore glorify God in your body and in your spirit, which are God's."* (1Corinthians 6:19-20)

"So now, brethren, I commend you to God and to the word of His grace, which is able to build you up and give you an inheritance among all those who are sanctified." (Acts 20:32)

This has now become your life's purpose. Don't look back! You have made the biggest decision of your life to follow Jesus and rebuild your life on this foundation; you will now regularly have to make smaller decisions in order to stick to it. Though the devil, the world and your flesh will try to persuade you to turn around, stay close to Jesus. *"I am the vine, you are the branches. He who abides in Me, and I in him, bears much fruit; for without Me you can do nothing."* (John 15:5) When we believe, and follow Him, the thirst in us that yearns for our Maker is quenched with living water. As we receive it, we are also able to give it to others around us. *"Whoever believes in Me, as the Scripture has said, streams of living water will flow from within him."* (John 7:38)

As a believer now you are entitled to tap into all God's promises, so start doing it!

On Earth Jesus demonstrated His authority over: Sickness: Disability: Nature: Satan: Demons: Sin and Death.
Now in Heaven He reigns over all, Commander in Chief of Heaven and the Universe; King of Kings and Lord of Lords.
Only subject to His Father and our Father, the Great I AM, the ALMIGHTY.

The Position

"you also, as living stones, are being built up a spiritual house,"
(1 Peter 2:5)

Now that our spirit has been regenerated by the Spirit of our God, it has to become stronger through reading and listening to the Word and by having fellowship with God and with our brothers and sisters in Christ. It has to take dominion over our whole being. We have to resist the flesh, the world and the devil, who latches onto the flesh like an octopus. Our position is in Christ, and our Father sees us as He sees Jesus. *"A voice came from heaven which said, 'You are My Beloved Son; in You I am well pleased.'"* (Luke 3:22). We are now His beloved sons and daughters, inside Jesus as He is inside us, so we are to build our sanctuary according to His template. We build it individually and together as a dwelling place for God through the Holy Spirit. To help understand this better, listen to **"Lord prepare me to be a Sanctuary"** on YouTube.

Christian communities (congregations) should be joyous, vibrant, loving and forgiving; looking forward to eternity rather than fearing it. We should, however, not forget that though we are in the world and sharing our existence with humanity, we are different from the world and should not try to do as they do – they can do it much better! This is not to say that there are not lovely people in the world from whom we can learn a lot about life, relationships and caring, but we have a God that wants us to be holy as He is. The Spirit of God is not called the Holy Spirit in vain. It should be our joy to be holy like our Lord. Holiness for us means to be consecrated and set aside for Him under all circumstances. This is not easy in a world that demands our compliance, but as long as we stay close to Jesus He helps us through.

Our salvation is the result of what Christ has done for us on the Cross, and nobody can boast. It is the foundation on which each person needs to build his or her life for God's Kingdom. If you build to the best of your ability by His power and His grace, you will receive your reward.

To be the best person you can be need not be a selfish ambition if your goal is to glorify God and help others. We have been created by God for His glory. He wants us to use what He has given us to the best of our ability to prepare us for eternity, with our treasures in Heaven waiting for us. To ask Him to help us accumulate treasures in heaven is more important than anything we can ask from Him or He can give to us. Of course, the greatest treasure we have is that our names are written in heaven. This is our starting point. This should also be the source of our greatest joy, even when all other reasons to be joyful fail us. "However, do not rejoice that the spirits submit to you, but rejoice that your names are written in heaven." (Luke 10:20)

He does not suppress our personalities, as people may try to tell you; on the contrary, loving Him and loving others as oneself, makes us become the people we were intended to be, free from self-centeredness, which is a major cause of unhappiness for ourselves and the people around us.

What is the foundation of our faith? First of all, it is our belief in Jesus Christ; His birth, His life and His words, His death, His resurrection, His ascension and His return. And then if we look at all the wonderful things around us and at ourselves – the music we can make, the songs we can sing, the things we can create – surely we must have been created wonderfully too? Though the story of creation in the Bible is not intended as a history book, God very clearly presents it to us in a way that we can understand. His description fills a gap in world history at a time from when no history books are available. In their endeavour to hide their own ignorance, people have tried to force the Bible into the position of a history book and then, from that arbitrary position, come up with issues about its validity.

If, for the sake of understanding what God tells us in His word, we forget the arguments about how this could have happened – nobody else was there to tell us anyway – and listen to what He says, this is what we learn. In the beginning, He created the world and all that is in it. Then He created mankind in His image and gave them authority over all He had made. Mankind forfeited this authority by listening to Satan instead of to God, and Satan took authority for himself. He has ruled the world in his own chaotic way, priding himself on establishing the modern world order with 'enlightened man' who no longer believes in God or in the Bible, but worships his own achievements. There is nothing wrong with scientific and technological knowledge – like everything else it is the gift of God – but viewing belief in Him as a crutch for the simple-minded is a fatal mistake, overshadowing all the good that may come out of such knowledge and practice.

In the meantime, God has His own way of shaping the history of this world. After Adam, there were people like Enoch, Noah, Abraham and David, through which He continued to work His plan. Through many tribulations He protected the nation of Israel, which eventually, through Mary, birthed His Son as the Son of Man.

The supernatural life of Jesus Christ is documented by reliable witnesses. Apart from the fact that He split the course of history in two, many details of His life were the fulfilling of Old Testament prophesies which were documented long before He came to live on Earth. There are many supernatural healings described in detail, as well as raising people from the dead and calming storms. Then, also, there is the supernatural change of life for someone who becomes a believer. Millions of people can testify to this. There are the testimonies of people with drug and other addictions who were immediately set free when they accepted Jesus Christ as their Saviour. This happens by the power of the Holy Spirit and cannot possibly happen naturally, though God blesses natural ways to help people as well.

Before we start considering practical ways that will help us grow, we have to understand our aim.

1. We want to grow in our total surrender to God and His will. This includes getting rid of any bondage to something else in our lives. Taking on the yoke of full surrender makes the Christian walk easier and if you do not surrender fully, it makes life most difficult. *"Come to Me, all you who labour and are heavy laden, and I will give you rest. Take My yoke upon you and learn from Me, for I am gentle and lowly in heart, and you will find rest for your souls. For My yoke is easy and My burden is light."* (Matthew 11:28-30) If we come out from under his yoke, many other yokes will come to rest on us. If we run back under his yoke they will be left behind, waiting for us, but let them wait! The yoke that Jesus talks about is also when we walk under "the fear of the Lord" instead of under" the fear of man," which is a snare. *"The fear of the Lord leads to life; then one rests content, untouched by trouble."* (Proverbs 19:23)

Derek Prince summarised the basics of living under an attitude of reverence for the Lord, in a radio message:

- Diligence (Proverbs 10:4)
- Confession (1John 1:9)
- Approach the throne of grace for mercy (Heb 4:16)
- Move on to maturity (Hebrews 10:19-22)
- Draw near to the most holy place (Heb 10:19-22)
- Without wavering (Hebrews 10:23)
- Consider one another (Hebrews 10:24)
- Endurance (Galatians 6)
- Gratitude, thankfulness (Hebrews 12:28-29)
- Willing to identify with Jesus (Hebrews 13:13)
- Sacrifice of praise continually (Hebrews 13:15)

2. We want to grow in total surrender to sharing what we have – money, possessions, time – with the less privileged, beginning with the household of God, but also in general. In this regard, we must remember that, as we look after the needs of others, God will look after our needs. We cannot out-give God!

Anyway, the things we have are not really ours, as we can lose them all in a moment. The surrendering of our life to Jesus, includes ourselves, and everything that belongs to us, as the saying goes, 'lock, stock and barrel.' *"...whoever of you does not forsake all that he has cannot be My disciple."* (Luke 14:33)

However, God gives us money and possessions to manage for Him, and we should do so diligently *"He who is faithful in what is least is faithful also in much; and he who is unjust in what is least is unjust also in much."* (Luke 16:10) so that when we leave here, to the measure that we looked after His Earthly belongings, He will give us our eternal belongings. *"And if you have not been faithful in what is another man's, who will give you what is your own?"* (Luke 16:12) *"...but lay up for yourselves treasures in heaven, where neither moth nor rust destroys and where thieves do not break in and steal."* (Matthew 6:20)

God also said that we should not do our good deeds to seen by men but in secret, then He will reward us. Remember that He sees the difficult situation you have to handle, even if nobody else knows about it. And we don't do good works to be rewarded by people. I once read a book about the life of St Theresa of Lisieux, where she mentioned that she would thank the Lord every time she did something for someone who did not give her as much as a thank you for it, and that it actually meant more to her than when she was thanked or praised for something. She would also thank God when others used something she had said to get credit for themselves. She had learned the secret to keep on loving the unlovable. The Lord put on her heart to really love someone as unlovable as you can get, with word and deeds. She relates that one day this person asked her, "What is there in me that makes you love me so much?"

When you are looking for a spouse, it is most important to find someone who shares the same values as you, otherwise he or she will be a bondage to you. If you cannot find such a person, rather stay alone if you are serious about your spiritual growth. If you are already married to someone who does not share your values, you can agree as to what belongs to each individually, then do with yours as you believe God wants you to. The principle here is to love others as you love yourself.

The more things there are in your life that you depend on, the less you will be able to come to total surrender and so enjoy God's blessing). We are inclined to look at the sacrifice and not comprehend the blessing, as the young man in (Mark 10:21-30) did. We know Jesus loves us all, but three persons whom the Bible specifically mentions as being loved by Him, are *"the disciple He loved"* (John 13:23) Lazarus (John 11:3) and this rich young man, who chose his belongings above Jesus. He could have been great in the Kingdom, but now we do not even know his name. How sad after all his hard work to be a good man, he had no treasure in Heaven! There was also Zacchaeus the tax collector (Luke 19:1-10) who freely offered to give half his possessions to the poor. Jesus did not say to him, "Give it all and come with Me" but left him offering quadruple recompense to anyone he had wronged out of what remained.

Just a question to anyone from another belief or religion who is reading this book; maybe you are extremely dedicated, and your earthly treasure is being a good person. Won't you listen to the call of Jesus, who loves you, to leave the 'riches' of your religion or belief/unbelief behind and follow Him?

If we think of Jacob (Genesis 32:26-28), he sacrificed his hip in his struggle for a blessing, which he received along with a new name. The sacrifice God may expect of us is very individual, but He will always help us to get rid of bondages, as nothing is impossible for Him (Mark 10:27).

A bicycle for one man may be a stronger bondage than an expensive sports car for another. Money was clearly not a bondage for the rich man, Joseph of Arimathea (Matthew 27:57-60). He wasn't asked to sell all his possessions but he willingly sacrificed to Jesus the new tomb which he had cut out for himself. Do you want to be loved by God for giving, listen to this: *"So let each one give as he purposes in his heart, not grudgingly or of necessity; for God loves a cheerful giver."* (2 Corinthians 9:7)

Maybe we should find a way to start sharing the things in our house that we do not use, and then go on to the things we can do without if there is someone in our congregation who needs them more than us. I know we can take things to the charity shop and that is good, but we are encouraged to start with our brothers and sisters. As times of persecution increase, sharing will help us survive. *"The people asked him, saying, 'What shall we do then'" He (John the Baptist) answered and said to them, 'He who has two tunics, let him give to him who has none; and he who has food, let him do likewise.'"* (Luke 3:10-11)

The following are ten important ways to strengthen your new life.

1. Learn to know God as your Father by doing His will and having a relationship with Him through your position in Jesus.
2. Read the Word of God, the Bible. Meditate on it, speak it and do it.
3. Pray: Take some time out of your daily schedule to talk with God. As His child, you can talk normally to Him. You can talk to Him any time, for instance, during your lunch break or when you're walking home – just don't shut your eyes as some people think they must do when they talk to God!
4. Join up with other believers, get baptized and partake in communion. Jesus said that even if only two or three are together in His name, there He will be also among them.
   Make sure that the church you join is centred around God and his Word and not around the opinions and desires of the world and of its members.
5. Ask God to allow the Holy Spirit to fill you with power or ask someone in authority to pray with you in order for you to be an effective witness.
6. Ask God for help to accomplish your goals and fulfil your needs. God answers our prayers when He knows the time is right. This may not be how or when we think it should be, but rest assured He wants the best for us.

7. Work to earn, to be independent and have some money to help others in need. Work is blessed by God as long as it is done diligently.

8. Take time to care for others and do good whenever you are in the position to do so. Nobody else has to know what you do, "*...but the Father who sees in secret will reward you.*" (Matthew 6:4)

9. To be a disciple you have to have a disciplined life. Not all people like this word, but order in your life is necessary for your growth as a Christian. This includes your daily program, your finances and how you relate to others.

10. Walk in victory over sin. The blood of Jesus cleanses us from sin and releases us from the bondage of sin. Our 'default mode' should now be that we do not want to sin ('must not' has turned into 'want not') and though Jesus has already paid the price for all our sins, past and present it does not give us the right to continue doing what is wrong. Rather we should ask for forgiveness and ask Him to help us to overcome. Jesus' blood was shed to take away our sins.

We have to take responsibility for what we think, say and do. There are nonetheless several weaknesses and temptations to which we are likely to be subject and which we should keep taking to the Cross until they are no longer a bondage. Continue to be careful, as the enemy may wait for another opportunity to encourage you to slip back. These weaknesses can include overindulgence in food, alcohol or sex, including watching pornography and compulsive masturbation. Any or all of these can lead to a bondage, which needs to be broken in order for you to be set free.

After all this, maybe we should say something about the word sin. Sin can be defined in other ways, but it is basically deviation from God's will and intention. Remember that pride was Satan's original sin. As soon as we get something right, his strategy is to entice us to succumb to pride. To combat pride, we must remember where we come from and that we are what we are only by God's grace, and ponder these words of Paul: *"But God forbid that I should boast except in the cross of our Lord Jesus Christ, by whom the world has been crucified to me, and I to the world."* (Galatians 6:14)

Satan and his demons will try to tell you that God is there to spoil your life. On the contrary, He is the only true giver of all the real joys we can experience on Earth. *"But let the righteous be glad; let them rejoice before God; Yes, let them rejoice exceedingly!"*
(Psalm 68:3) How complete will our joy be in Heaven with all that is happening there!

Now, back to Earth; within the limits of His love for us and surrounded by His wisdom, we are free – our freedom only limited by the freedom of those around us. In this regard, we can experience: the joy of worshipping our God and experiencing His presence; the joy of his peace, *"Peace I leave with you, My peace I give to you; not as the world gives do I give to you. Let not your heart be troubled, neither let it be afraid."* (John 14:27) The joy of seeking His Kingdom to come; the joy of getting rid of guilt; the joy of children and to be part of a family, the joy of food and wine, of looking at His creation, of fulfilment and salvation; the joy of being filled with the Holy Spirit, the joy of friendship; love and sex. (Sex was God's idea, and without it life on Earth as we know it would have become extinct, or never existed. Sadly, perversion makes it destructive, especially when lust for sex and money come together.)

"The joy of the Lord is your strength." (Nehemiah 8:10)

Come on, with all these joys in store for you, why would you still listen to the devil? What can he offer you? Maybe riches and fame and happiness that doesn't last? But definitely selfishness, false freedom, lies, fear, hate, pride, jealousy, drunkenness and headaches, drug dependency and dealing, empty sex and STDs, the abuse of children and others, murder, terrorism and war, sickness and pain. None of these will you find in Heaven.

On the Earth, we also see natural disasters and famine, which followed after Man sinned against God, (Genesis 3:17-19). Despite the fact that mankind handed the reins of power over to Satan, we still blame God if things go wrong, like Adam blaming God for his sin. *"Then the man said, 'The woman whom you gave to be with me, she gave me of the tree, and I ate.'"*(Genesis 3:12) And at the beginning of the relationship, that same Adam was so excited about her! Is this not how things happen in our own relationships – whatever is wrong, it is usually the other person's fault?

According to God's warning and against Satan's lie, death followed sin, of which the first death was murder, but then, seemingly an aging factor was introduced into the DNA, and all subsequent attempts to combat aging have so far produced limited results, in spite of billions being invested in research.

Did you know that the one thing that will strengthen our faith more than any other is to be a witness for Him? As we prepare ourselves to do His work we must be prayerfully ready to seize every opportunity to share with others the great things God has done for us. As we go along, we must look forward to the opportunities He gives us, rather than thinking of this as a burden. Witnessing is also a way for believers to connect with one another and strengthen their faith.

Apart from witnessing locally, you may ask, how can we fulfil our part in the Great Commission by doing missionary work? There are still many missionary opportunities if we look for them, like YWAM (Youth with a Mission). Their motto is, *"To know God and to make Him known"*. Of course you do not have to go anywhere else than where you are to make this *your* life goal, but we can go to countries where the Gospel still needs to be proclaimed – according to statistics there are about 865 million people unreached by the Gospel, mainly in predominantly Muslim countries where it is, however, rather dangerous to go and do missionary work. Some of these people are coming to us as migrants, and in that way the mission field is coming to us, instead of us going there.

We can now, in peaceful circumstances, introduce them to Jesus, whom they never have had the opportunity to hear about or the freedom to consider following.

But are we doing this? And for how long will it still be possible? The devil has been planning ahead in his quest to try and prevent these people becoming Christians; he thought of a clever way to discourage people from evangelising, by starting to put up barriers. First of all, it is now generally seen that "religion is something private" and should not be discussed. "We should just accept one another's religions" or be politically correct, even if we can help them not to experience Judgement Day. The word 'evangelize' is being equated to 'proselytize' a word which doesn't sound good, in order to discourage Christians from bringing the good news of the Gospel to others. Lately the words 'extremist' and 'fundamentalist' are being used more frequently – at first in the context of Muslim radicalisation, but creeping into discussions about Christianity. The devil wants to stop Christians bringing the Gospel by classifying it as an act of extremism. It may even become against the law to evangelize here, as has already happened in some other countries. *"How then shall they call on Him in whom they have not believed? And how shall they believe in Him of whom they have not heard? And how shall they hear without a preacher?"* (Romans 10:14)

The Government must, of course, do whatever they can to stop acts of terrorism, but we have to be free to present the Gospel of Jesus Christ to all people, including radicalised extremists. We may think it is impossible for them to turn and follow Jesus, but with God everything is possible, and the power of the Cross is stronger to set men and women free than any other power that may bind them.

"And Jesus came and spoke to them, saying, 'All authority has been given to Me in heaven and on earth. Go therefore and make disciples of all the nations, baptizing them in the name of the Father and of the Son and of the Holy Spirit, teaching them to observe all things that I have commanded you; and lo, I am with you always, even to the end of the age.'" (Matthew 28:18-20)

"...that at the name of Jesus every knee should bow, of those in heaven, and of those on earth, and of those under the earth, and that every tongue should confess that Jesus Christ is Lord, to the glory of God the Father." (Philippians 2:10-11)

The Power

*"And the disciples were filled with joy and with the
Holy Spirit"* (Acts 13:52)

The Holy Spirit uses the blood of Jesus to cleanse us and
to remove our sins. He fills our lives and brings the Joy of
the Lord to our hearts – a happiness that surpasses any
other feelings offered by persons, things, drugs or drink.

*"Do not be drunk with wine, in which is dissipation; but
be filled with the Spirit,"* (Ephesians 5:18)

When Jesus ascended to Heaven, He promised to ask the
Father to send us a helper to be with us and encourage us.
This helper is the Holy Spirit, Who next to salvation is the
greatest gift He could give to His church and to all those

who choose to follow Him. He makes true Christianity supernatural otherwise it could easily become just another set of rules. Jesus, the Son of God, was born through Mary to be the Son of Man. We, the sons and daughters of man, are born through that same Holy Spirit to become God's children.

"But as many as received Him, to them He gave the right to become children of God, to those who believe in His name:" (John 1:12)

Jesus said that, for us to be effective witnesses, we need to be empowered by the Holy Spirit, who will also guide and remind us of Jesus' words. It is the Holy Spirit who creates among us the love and unity that is the trademark of those who follow Jesus. *"By this all will know that you are My disciples, if you have love for one another."* (John 13:35)

The Holy Spirit uses the blood of Jesus to cleanse us and to remove our sins.

How do we receive the Holy Spirit? When we become Christians we receive Him, but we have to seek Him more, to receive His power. Keep on praying or ask someone to pray for you. The baptism of the Holy Spirit can happen instantly, but there are people who had the infilling of the Holy Spirit at their conversion, and the Spirit has grown stronger in their lives as they followed Jesus with total dedication. Someone may say, if the Holy Spirit is our Comforter, then why don't we experience His presence on the many occasion when we need Him? The answer is we experience Him only as we 'walk in the Spirit.' When we walk our own way or if we walk 'in the flesh' we won't experience Him. As we go forward for the cause of the Kingdom, we are refreshed by the Holy Spirit, as the Psalmist said of the Lord on his way to victory. *"He shall drink of the brook by the wayside; therefore He shall lift up the head."* (Psalm 110:7)

When things go wrong for us, the devil can understand that we get frustrated and angry. He can understand when we rebuke him for it or blame God (which he likes) or that we become despondent, or doubt our faith (which is actually what he wants) What he cannot understand is when God's children still walk in victory, and keep on drinking from the brook and lift up their heads against him, in spite of anything he and the world can throw at them.

It is by the power of the Holy Spirit that the Church was established and God still enables His children to be His witnesses. *"But you shall receive power when the Holy Spirit has come upon you; and you shall be witnesses to Me in Jerusalem, and in all Judea and Samaria, and to the end of the earth."* (Acts 1:8)

The Church, still imperfect in many ways, represents Christ, as His body on Earth, and is also referred to in Scripture as His Bride. Christianity as a religion experiences ebb and flow, but the universal Church, consisting of devout members whose names are written in the Book of Life, and who are present in all true Christian denominations, will only get stronger as it is more refined by persecution. Many devout members of the Moslem faith will acknowledge Jesus as the Son of the living God by revelation and then many more by their witnessing. In the same way, Israel, will eventually accept Jesus as their Messiah and all believers will become One. Then the Bride of Christ, consisting of the redeemed throughout all the ages, will manifest herself in glory, ready for the wedding feast of the Lamb!

Besides the removal of sin from the world and the resurrection of the dead, we look forward to the new creation that God promised, when the present dispensation will come to an end. Until such time we as His children must move forward in the power of His Kingship to bring the message of Salvation to all people, and to encourage, support and strengthen those who believe. As the song goes: *"Everybody ought to know who Jesus is…"*

Prelude

We have to remember that when time ends, things need no longer happen in chronological order, and material things that which we observe now will go

Before the New Dispensation comes fully into being, Jesus will come back, the dead will all rise followed by Judgement Day. Gods children will stay with Him for ever and the others will join the devil to go to the place prepared for him.

"But the day of the Lord will come as a thief in the night, in which the heavens will pass away with a great noise, and the elements will melt with fervent heat; both the earth and the works that are in it will be burned up." (2 Peter 3:10)

The new dispensation

The new Earth, now in the same dimension as Heaven, which is indestructible, will come forward.

The Kingdom of God or, as it is also called, the Kingdom of Heaven will totally engulf and rule the Earth, which would now be suitable for being united with Heaven.

Then we will experience reality.

"Now I saw a new heaven and a new earth, for the first heaven and the first earth had passed away. Also there was no more sea." (Revelation 21:1)

The new Earth will be as wonderful as Heaven. The New Jerusalem will come from heaven and unite with the spiritual dimension of the present Jerusalem, and God will live on earth with His people and be their light. There will most probably be picturesque rivers and lakes, but all so much wonderful than I can ever describe.

"Eye has not seen, nor ear heard, nor have entered into the heart of man, the things which God has prepared for those who love Him." (1 Corinthians 2:9) We know for sure about one river that will be there: *"And he showed me a pure river of water of life, clear as crystal, proceeding from the throne of God and of the Lamb."* (Revelation 22:1)

There will be peace and great harmony between all people, between God and the people, and between the people and the land, (Greenpeace will not be needed to fight for the environment, though they will get their reward for their endeavours to protect God's world). And God's glory will be everywhere. *"For the earth, will be filled with the knowledge of the glory of the Lord, as the waters cover the sea"* (Habakkuk 2:14).

Don't you feel like shouting with me?

PRAISE GOD. HALLELUJAH!

The Testimony

The picture above, which was drawn by my grandson when he was still very young, clearly depicts the covering hand of God, protecting a small boat on its way to a city. There was a very similar picture on a tract I once received from a crippled old man, to whom I will refer later.

I would like to share this testimony because it is one which I firmly believe and also live by. I want to share it; as someone who is entrusted with a great treasure, which he wishes to share with all mankind and does not want to keep to himself. I do so with humility and respect to all.

Though I was brought up in a Christian home, as a young person I did not share the Christian faith and so did not want to have anything to do with the God that people told me about.

Rebellious and without any friends, I was sent by my parents to a boarding school, where I at first had friends who were like me, much to the disappointment of my mother who would continue to pray for me. Then three things happened to me, one after the other.

I went home for the holidays. When the train pulled out of a station along the way, the conductor slipped and fell and his head was crushed in the gap between the train and the platform. The train came to a stand-still and we all got out. I stood there in the small crowd and was looking on as they carried the dead man away, *when a man put his hand on my shoulder and said,* "I tried to talk to that man about his soul a short while ago, but he wouldn't listen to me."

After getting home I went to the 'bioscope', which was the name used for the cinema then. An old man who was crippled, sitting on the steps next to the entrance, gave me a piece of paper with a picture on it and words that described, *'The Way to Salvation.'* Uninterested, I did not look at it, yet for some reason I could not bring myself to throw it away. Later that evening, I removed it from my pocket and decided to look at it. There was a picture of a man in a boat on a journey towards a beautiful city. Though the sea was rough I thought to myself that surely, he would make it because of the large hand which stretched over the boat protecting him. It suddenly it struck me that if I were that man in the boat I probably would not have the hand of God to protect me because I did not believe in Him. I also gave thought of the man on the train.

That Sunday my parents invited me to church to listen to the evangelist Oswald Smith. I was half asleep but heard the man say something like, "If you want to give God a chance in your life, please put up your hand." I thought to myself 'God will not be able to say one day I that didn't give Him a chance' and I put up my hand. Then he asked those who had put up their hands to stand up and asked us to come forward. Apart from me many others went forward and we were all sobbing! Later I realised that we were under the conviction of the Holy Spirit.

It was on that day I accepted Jesus Christ as my Lord and Saviour. This was almost sixty years ago, and, though it was extremely difficult at the beginning and I was even doubtful about my faith for a while. At first, I think I did not fully surrender and it was hard to keep faith. One Sunday morning in a small country church, it all changed; while we were singing the hymn *'Just as I am without one plea…'* I said "Lord here am I, fully giving myself to You, holding back nothing, I don't want any other yokes to carry, only yours." *"Take my yoke upon you and learn from me, for I am gentle and humble in heart, and you will find rest for your souls"* (Matthew 11:29)

Soon I felt led to join a group of 'on-fire-for-the-Lord' young people and I still remember the day we went camping and traveling in a closed removal truck. They sang songs like *'Everybody ought to know who Jesus is'* and the Afrikaans song *'O goedheid Gods hier nooit vol prese'* in different tones of voice – I thought I could just as well have been in Heaven!

I know this was my 'First Love' experience with the Lord and I always go back to it when I feel I am losing some of my fire. It was so easy to be a child of God and a witness for Him. During this time of spiritual awakening my wife, Linda, also met the Lord in a nearby town, years before we knew each other. She has related to me how she was running and singing in the meadow after she gave her heart to Jesus, as I am sure she will do again one day in Heaven, and then we will run together.

I have never had any regrets about surrendering myself to Jesus. This marked a turning point in my life as it was only then that I decided to attend Medical School, and go and work in a mission hospital. I started to study hard to improve my school results, which I needed to do to be admitted as a medical student, and the Lord helped me.

In my walk with Jesus, there are two experiences, of many, which I would like to tell you about.

It was a rather dark evening, and my wife and I had just attended a meeting at a place called Kwasizabantu in Kwazulu-Natal, South Africa. The Spirit of God was working wonders at the place but, as we discovered that night, the devil was also active. We were shown to a little hut, separate from the main buildings, where we could stay the night. Linda felt uneasy immediately and wanted us to go somewhere else, but I didn't feel that was the right thing to do, and said we could go in the morning. I think that disagreement between the two of us left an opening for the enemy. *"Husbands, in the same way be considerate as you live with your wives, treat them with respect as the weaker partner and as heirs with you in the gracious gift of life, so that nothing will hinder your prayers."* (1 Peter 3:7)

After we entered the hut I saw something that looked like five black mice crawling in from the door side, I went nearer with the lantern, but couldn't see them again. Linda went off to sleep and, as I was preparing for bed, the wind started to blow so hard that the whole hut was shaking. When I put out the lantern and lay down on the bed, I felt as though something was trying to choke the life out of me. Three thoughts came to my mind over and over again, "You are going to die!" and "There is no God! The bible is not true."

I responded by saying, "I believe with all my heart there is a God!" By this time the wind had become even stronger. In the dark, I got hold of my little flashlight and my Bible and, with shivering hands, open the Bible and shone the light exactly onto John 17:17 which says: *"Sanctify them by the truth, your word is truth."*

"Yes," I said, "I stake my life on it! 'Gods word is the truth'" As I said those words, the 'thing' that was throttling me let go and, just as suddenly as the wind started, it calmed down totally and I went into a restful sleep.

Is there anybody who will try to convince me that this was only my imagination? Or that, as a medical doctor, I wouldn't know if it was a hallucination? Never! And what are the chances that I would open the Bible and shine my little flashlight on exactly the right words for the situation in which I found myself – words that gave me the power to overcome?

One evening I was standing on the beach all by myself. I asked the Lord "It is so quiet and lonely; can't you just send an angel to come and talk to me? That will really strengthen my faith."
All that came were the breakers, one after the other, and the moon was shining on the water, and a soft wind was blowing through my hair. Then I understood that if I take in what I see and hear, I know this is the work of His hands, and He has given us His word. He reminded me about His words to Thomas: *"Jesus said to him, 'Thomas, because you have seen Me, you have believed. Blessed are those who have not seen and yet have believed.'"* (John 20:29)

I must admit I do not consider myself perfect – far from it. However, one thing I am sure of, is I know that I am forgiven for my sins and have a hope for an eternal life. That Name that so many of us, including myself in my earlier years, use so lightly and would take away from its true meaning had become my Saviour. Moreover, I am comforted by the promise that if I follow His teachings and hold on to my faith to the end, I will have a place, prepared for me, in Heaven!

"For God so loved the world that He gave His one and only Son, that whoever believes in Him shall not perish but have eternal life." (John 3:16)

Eternal life does not start when you die, it starts the moment you receive Christ as your Lord and Saviour. Once you have done this all your sins are forgiven and you are ready to receive His Spirit. I will admit the walk with Jesus can be difficult but never dull. In fact, it is more exciting than anything you can imagine... and the best thing is, it never ends!

God's way of calling can be different for each one of us. This testimony is about how He called me – for someone else it may just be a word or a situation, or He may call you as you are reading now!

As I am moving on in years, I also move forward in the queue to depart from this world and go to my eternal home. We are all afraid of the pain or whatever else may precede it, but I am not afraid of death. *"Death has been swallowed up in victory ... "* (1 Corinthians 15:54) I am actually excited as I am looking forward to seeing my God face to face and falling at my Saviour's feet, thanking Him for His great salvation. And I know that, on that day, the tears of persecution and suffering of all those around me will have been turned into tears of joy.

The Lord has given me a poem based on Psalm 18:35 *"You give me Your shield of victory, and Your right hand sustains me; You stoop down to make me great."*

The King of the universe looked down to the Earth,
the place of His suffering and shame
When for others' transgressions He took the blame.
Amongst the rubble of broken lives,
He saw something move; was there someone alive?
Then when He stooped down, He saw it was me
And He picked me up though I first tried to flee.
But when I looked up in His eyes I could see
The love that made Him die also for me.
He took me and held me close to His heart
And apart from clean clothes gave me a new start
He stooped down once more to put me in place
where again I became part of the human race
And when as His witness my time will be done
He will take me to where there's no need for the sun.

(Revelation 22:5)

Just a Book has a dual purpose:

1. To inform and encourage unbelievers to become believers.
2. To inform and encourage believers to become disciples.

If you found this book useful, I think you will also enjoy reading my other book, *The Wonder of the New Birth* from Amazon or Lulu.com. There is also *I Will Be the Best Me I Can Be Second Edition Revised* a handbook for adults with ADHD, which contains the footprints of God's unmentioned presence.

Editing by Diane Morrison
Illustrations by Dawn Larder

All profits from the selling this book will go towards its free distribution and to helping people in need.

24499520R00047

Printed in Great Britain
by Amazon